A Twyford Cardinal
flat-topped table
washbasin supported
in a mahogany
cabinet with tiled
splashback and
mirror. This basin
was fitted at
Thomas Twyford's
home at Biddulph
Moor, Staffordshire.

Bathroom Ceramics

Munroe Blair

A Shire book

Published in 2002 by Shire Publications Ltd,
Cromwell House, Church Street, Princes Risborough,
Buckinghamshire HP27 9AA, UK.
(Website: www.shirebooks.co.uk)

British Library Cataloguing in Publication Data:
Blair, Munroe
Bathroom ceramics. – (A Shire album; 391)
1. Bathrooms – Great Britain – History
2. Ceramic industries – Great Britain – History
I. Title 747.7'8
ISBN 0 7478 0513 X

Cover: *A composite of illustrations demonstrating the development, type variation, material and decoration of ceramic sanitaryware. The items featured include a Spode bone china bowl and ewer, and an Edward Johns earthenware washbasin decorated with marbleised and floral transfers plus hand-painted details. Twyford's white interior fireclay bath has a cream glazed upstand, shelf and exterior with raised decoration detailed in white.*

ACKNOWLEDGEMENTS
I am indebted to the many people whose expertise has contributed towards ensuring the historical accuracy of this book. Everyone's help has been sincerely appreciated. The extensive help given by the following individuals and organisations deserves special mention: Clare Briegal and Terry Woolliscroft on Doulton and Twyford brands, for photographic help and archive research; Angela Lee, Gladstone Working Pottery Museum, for her patience and co-operation; Roger Cooper, Ideal-Standard; David Woodcock, National Museum of Science and Industry; Ruth Brown, Staffordshire University Slide Library; Simon Kirkby, Thomas Crapper Collection; Pam Woolliscroft, Spode Museum Trust; Miranda Goodby, The Potteries Museum and Art Gallery; Ann Steedman, Heritage Services, Bath; Luitwin Gisberg von Boch-Galhau, Villeroy & Boch; Gaye Blake Roberts and the dedicated Wedgwood Museum team; Sam Woodberry, Armitage Shanks. Last, but not least, I thank Margaret, my patient wife, and Professor Colin Reeves, who combined to form my personal proofreading team.

Printed in Malta by Gutenberg Press Limited, Gudja Road,
Tarxien PLA 19, Malta.

Contents

Note: for ease of reference, terms and names that are explained in the glossary on page 38 are printed in italic type when they first occur in the text.

Twyfords' No. J35 earthenware 'Athena' lavatory, size 27 by 21 inches (68 by 53 cm), with gunmetal hot and cold taps, 'Sola' lift-up control knob waste and overflow fitting, twin brass towel rails, and painted cast-iron stand, shelf and frame including a bevelled plate-glass mirror. This total assembly was priced in Twyfords' January 1911 J Catalogue at £5 8s.

Civilisation, hygiene and ceramics

The earliest settled agricultural communities were made up of pioneer farmers who dwelt alongside running water or freshwater lakes for washing, cooking, drinking and crop irrigation. From the fourth millennium BC early civilisations such as the Sumerians and Babylonians of Mesopotamia, the Egyptians, the Minoans of Crete, the Indus Valley civilisation and the Chinese have benefited from sophisticated hydraulic sanitary engineering systems. The Romans adopted and adapted the health-protecting arrangements of these earlier societies to become the hydraulic engineering experts of the ancient world.

Above: *Sea-shell motifs recur in many baths and washbasin designs: this sculptured marble bath is displayed in Cuba's National Museum, Havana. (Author's drawing.)*

The Romans took the benefits of their hygiene and sanitary engineering expertise to the peoples they conquered. Their skill at collecting drinking and washing water from sources such as springs and wells played a major part in the Empire's success. The quality and abundance of clean water were vital factors in the Roman Empire's expansion and longevity. Each citizen of ancient Rome had over 1300 litres of water available for daily use, which illustrates the great importance this civilisation placed on pure water. After drinking and washing needs had been served waste water was channelled to flush excretion through sewers for disposal in rivers, lakes or the sea.

The conquering Romans brought the habits of washing, bathing and drinking clean water to Britain in the first century AD. Roman engineers located Britain's clean water sources and harnessed hot springs to supply prestigious communal bath buildings. In AD 54, within ten years of their arrival in western England, the Romans started building a bathing complex at *Aquae Sulis* (now Bath). When Roman legions withdrew from Britain in the fourth century, this and many other fully operable sanitary engineering projects were left behind.

Down the centuries monks maintained clean water for their communities for drinking and washing: the important religious discipline of washing before and after meals was practised in most English monasteries. In the mid fourteenth

In AD 54 Roman colonists started construction of the Aquae Sulis bathing complex over a natural hot spring in what became the city of Bath. (Bath and North East Somerset Heritage Services: photograph by Simon McBride.)

century the Black Death reduced England's population by a third but monastic communities, accustomed to better personal hygiene and clean drinking water, had higher than average survival rates. Henry VIII's dissolution of the monasteries in the 1530s resulted in their hydraulic engineering systems silting up or falling into disuse.

The purifying effects of water have for centuries been associated with religious rituals: Christians baptise new members by symbolically wetting an initiate's head or, for Baptists, partially or totally immersing the candidate; and during the Kumbh Mela festival millions of Hindu pilgrims immerse themselves for spiritual purification in the River Ganges.

Among the forerunners of ceramic bathrooms are marble or terracotta baths and precious metal bowls in which members of the ruling classes of ancient civilisations washed themselves. In the Middle Ages people washed in pewter, leather or baked clay washing bowls or buckets. Sixteenth-century meals began with a ritual cleansing of hands, but hand-washing was thought unnecessary in the seventeenth century, when dinner forks were introduced. Throughout the years Samuel Pepys kept his diary, from 1660 to 1669, Mrs Pepys is noted to have taken only one bath.

By the nineteenth century wash bason stands (as the term was then spelt) had become substantial items of bedroom furniture, usually with easy-to-clean flat marble or slate tops. At first, separate *ewers and bowls* for personal washing were placed on them. After this the bowls were recessed into the marble tops and water was supplied from taps, and wash bowls became available in more ambitious shapes and larger sizes and with various decorations. Up to the middle of the nineteenth century many tableware potters continued to make *toilet sets* as well as bowls for bidets, washstands and *water closets* (*WCs*). British pottery wash bowls were exported around the world, setting the standards for quality and reliability.

A Spode toilet set with ewer and bowl, soap, brush and sponge trays, water jug, jerry and washbowl; decorated under glaze in the B185 floral transfer pattern.

Above: *John Ridgway's pottery fountain hand basins exhibited at the 1851 Great Exhibition.*

The southern transept entrance to Paxton's Crystal Palace, built to house the 1851 Great Exhibition of the Works of Industry of all Nations.

The growth in demand for larger, more complicated *washbasins* and large baths fostered the emergence of the *sanitaryware* sector within the British ceramic industry. In 1848 Thomas Twyford opened the first factory dedicated to the production of washbasins and other sanitary pottery at Bath Street, Hanley, in Staffordshire.

One aim of the 1851 Great Exhibition was to establish worldwide free trade but this was hampered by economic and political upheaval in many countries over the next half century. Many European markets imposed import tariffs, making exported British goods uneconomical, and in order to avoid losing their profitable European sanitaryware business several English potters built factories in Germany.

By the end of the nineteenth century most of Britain's working-class population stood or squatted to bathe in galvanised metal tubs. To attract and retain a contented workforce, pioneer factory owners began to provide fixed bathrooms in workers' homes: conditions at Cadbury's Bournville and Lever's Port Sunlight model industrial villages gradually encouraged wider sanitary reform.

Lloyd George promised British troops returning from the First World War improved living conditions. The 'Homes for Heroes' had a bath, washbasin, WC and kitchen sink – to us minimal sanitary requirements, but a luxury still not available to many middle-class and most working-class families in the early twentieth century.

After the Second World War many nations with an adverse balance of payments began producing their own sanitaryware; British ceramic technicians assisted in the establishment of sanitaryware factories worldwide. Many civilised nations are now self-sufficient in sanitaryware production.

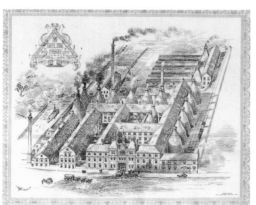

Twyford's Cliffe Vale factory, opened in 1887, providing healthy working conditions; each potter's work bench was by a window for the control of daylight and air flow.

The eighteenth century: age of elegance

Early washstands had removable bowls of copper, pewter or tin, or even silver or gold. Hand-painted porcelain bowls became available in France during the 1740s and under French influence elegant wash bason stands and bidets were introduced into the bedrooms of the English privileged classes in the 1750s. With the increasing popularity of personal hygiene, the British market for wash bowls grew.

After several years of royal patronage the Sèvres porcelain factory moved near to Versailles and Louis XV became sole proprietor in 1759. The Sèvres porcelain wash bowls were richly gilded and colourfully decorated to the royal taste and, although quite small, were outrageously expensive. Some precious metal and marble wash stand bowls were still made but the English nobility and gentry, following French taste and mindful of the patronage of Louis XV, favoured Sèvres decorated porcelain.

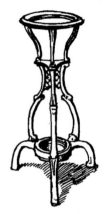

A mahogany bason stand to suit a metal or porcelain bowl, developed from the French 'lavemains' of the 1750s. (Author's drawing.)

In order to compete with the Sèvres wash bowls, English potters made bowls and toilet sets for wash stands. The tableware experience of British potters enabled them to respond with competitively priced decoration in a variety of bowl sizes. In the second half of the eighteenth century English potters offered hand-painted or transferred decoration on their pottery wash bowls. Those with fired-on transfer decoration were far less expensive than the French hand-enamelled porcelain or metal bowls. The average size of wash bowls was 15–18 inches (38–46 cm) in diameter and about 5 inches (12.5 cm) deep.

A Spode decorated bowl in Lange Lijsen underglaze transfer pattern, c.1820–33.

7

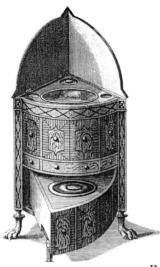

A Twyford 1809 panorama-decorated plug bowl, so called from the outlet plug to retain washing water, and developed from the small bowls used in early bason stands.

Left: *Sheraton's 1803 illustration of his 'Night Bason Stand', with holes for a pottery washing bowl and separate soap and sponge dishes. Below was a hinged cupboard concealing a chamber pot with lid, which could be swung outwards for use.*

Britain's wealthy society commissioned toilet tables from furniture designers such as Chippendale, Hepplewhite and Sheraton. Ewer and bowl sets were gradually replaced in richer homes by fixed wash bowls recessed flush into marble tops. Water 'on tap' was provided by means of a tank concealed within the cabinet above the bowl with a control valve; waste water discharged into a bucket beneath; this required emptying by hand.

The rest of the population washed in simple pottery bowls filled from a ewer. Water for washing was warmed by domestic staff before delivery to the user's dressing-room. These ewer and bowl combinations formed part of toilet sets and became popular with the middle and working classes for personal washing.

Many recessed washbasins were pivoted over a pottery *receiver* concealed in a cupboard below, and emptying instructions on the bowl's front edge directed users to 'lift'. The waste water poured into the receiver to drain away

Above: *A pottery cabinet table washbasin with marble splashback concealing a water tank. Water flow is controlled by moving the nozzle over the bowl or stopped when the nozzle is pushed towards the back. By twisting the front handle, waste water is discharged into a bucket concealed in the cupboard.*

A Spode portable white pottery bidet, complete with a mahogany support and cover to convert it into a stool. This type of bidet was typical of those used in the late eighteenth and early nineteenth centuries. Photographed in Spode's Blue Room Museum Trust Collection.

8

A Spode bidet, c.1814, decorated in Tower transfer pattern with brass waste.

through a waste pipe. These pivoted washbasins were known as *tip-up bowls*. The majority of them were in their turn replaced by *plug-bowl* washbasins.

The bidet was another French introduction. The term *bidet* means 'little horse': the user sits astride it to wash intimate areas. The earliest recorded use of a bidet was in 1710, when Madame de Prie granted audience to the Marquis d'Argenson while seated. Until bidets became *plumbed-in* fixtures, their bowls also had to be filled from ewers. Portable bidets were often concealed in pieces of furniture, with supporting legs and covers to disguise their use.

The aristocracy of some ancient civilisations had had baths with hot and cold running water and waste systems. Little had changed by the mid nineteenth century, when only the very wealthy could afford a plumbed-in bath. Workers for whom bathing was a necessity – coal miners and iron-foundry workers, for example – used portable metal tubs, usually in front of the kitchen fire for some degree of comfort in wintertime. These simple tubs allowed users enough space to stand or squat to wash down their bodies. The water had to be heated in the kitchen boiler, carried to the tub and emptied away after use. The main washing facility available in most homes remained a ewer and bowl.

Below left: *A galvanised tin bath used by manual workers.*

Below right: *A Wedgwood ewer and bowl set, c.1860, with transfer in Ningpo pattern.*

9

Plumbed-in fixtures

By the mid eighteenth century there was limited availability of pumped mains-pressure water, which made possible the filling of storage tanks in the roofs of some of the grander houses. Water tanks filled from the mains pipe, providing a constant supply of water for plumbed-in bidets, washbasins and very few baths. Roof-space tanks gave sufficient pressure by gravity to supply hot and cold water to some upper-floor bedrooms. The height of the roof tank and its remoteness from the plumbed-in fixtures determined the outlet pressure from the taps. Water was heated in boilers to feed the gravity system at Chatsworth House, Derbyshire, giving equally balanced pressure at hot and cold taps.

Washing tables with marble or slate tops were standard within most wealthy households. A popular Victorian choice was to recess marble or pottery bowls into marble-topped mahogany cabinets. Colourful wall tiles completed the grandeur of the bathroom décor. Wealthy Victorians designed large bathrooms with a bath and shower, bidet, washbasin and WC. Taps were fixed to walls, or through washing tabletops.

Left: *A bason stand with an inset marble bowl, in the Victoria and Albert Museum. Rather than discharging into a drainage system, waste water drained into a bucket in the cupboard below.*

Below: *A marble-topped mahogany washing-table unit, with a pottery bowl filled by a nozzle concealed behind a monkey-head shield. Water-control valves are mounted on the raised shelf with a plumbed-in supply and waste system.*

A page from a catalogue, showing folding tip-up lavatories (i.e. washbasins) suitable for bedrooms, ships and first-class railway carriages. Waste water tipped from the bowl as the hinged shelf was folded away.

From the 1850s effective mains water became more generally available, providing piped supplies to upper floors, but many Victorian households still relied on having their personal washing water brought and emptied by domestic staff. Many country houses of the landed gentry had separate water-supply tanks and receivers for the family's needs in each bedroom.

Gradually the use of the traditional washing bowls and ewers that had to be filled and emptied by hand declined. Toilet sets were replaced by fixed, plumbed-in water-supply and waste systems. When connected to supply and waste services, plug bowls were known as *fixtures*. Water was held in the wash bowl by a brass plug fitted into the waste outlet hole and anchored on to the work top by a chain. After washing, the user lifted the plug to drain away the waste water.

Along with the convenience of tap-controlled running water came the responsibility on users to turn the taps off when the wash bowl held sufficient water. Unaccustomed to having water 'on tap', Victorians often left taps open and this led to the introduction of overflows on plug bowls to prevent bathrooms from being flooded.

Cutting the holes for wash bowls subjected marble tops to the danger of breakage during preparation or when in use. To overcome the breakage problems, some marble slabs were cut through at their narrowest vulnerable sections, but the result left joints that were difficult to clean.

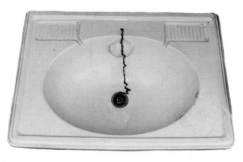

Above: *An earthenware flat-topped table washbasin by Edward Johns.*

Right: *A wash bowl with metal supply inlet concealed behind a monkey-head shield.*

Below: *Shells were also popular as inlet and overflow shields.*

Decorative sea shells or monkey or lion heads were popular features to disguise dual-purpose supply inlets and overflow outlets.

Even with water supplied from taps, recessed tip-up wash bowls continued in use and remained unchanged for many years. Where space was scarce in bedrooms, or on luxury ships and trains, elegant mahogany units with *folding tip-up washbasins* were introduced. The pottery wash bowl was fixed to a hinged shelf and, after use, the basin-supporting shelf was raised into a closed position, tipping water to a waste pipe. During the transitional period this type of washbasin was marketed as suitable for small concealed tanks or piped supplies.

Plumbed-in washing-table assemblies were often supported on elaborate mahogany furniture to match bedroom decor, and this made them affordable only by the wealthy. Marble worktops with ornate soap-tray recesses carved into the surface and separate anti-splash surrounds were also expensive. The junctions between the pottery bowl,

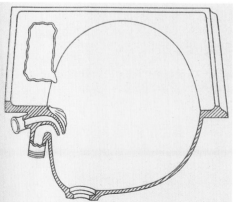

This section of Twyford's patent integral supply nozzle and overflow shows the spigots for connection to services.

Right: *An illustration of tip-up bowls and containers from Twyford's 1888 catalogue.*

Below: *A decorated flat-topped washing table to fit into a cabinet with water supplied from above.*

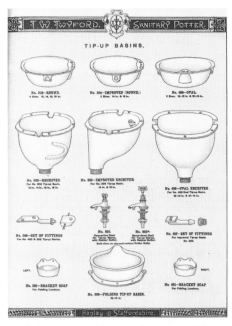

Left: *A flat-topped cabinet-stand washing table with blue and gold decoration.*

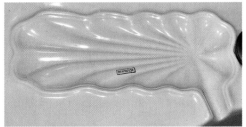

A scalloped and raised-rib soap tray, formed by pressing the clay into a plaster mould.

marble top and *upstand* were dirt traps. Not satisfied with supplying plug bowls only, sanitary potters had been making flat *table* washbasins since the mid nineteenth century to overcome the problem of joints. These one-piece ceramic washbasins emulated marble washing tables and incorporated an integral bowl with tray space complete with soap recesses. The result was the washbasin without joints between the bowl and tray. Recessed *wastes* and decoration further enhanced their appeal. Since the majority of washbasins were still supported on cabinets or cast-iron stands they were known as *cabinet stands*.

One improvement to the plug and chain was the secret overflow and waste outlet controlled by a lift-up knob on the tray, so that there was no need to put a hand back into the dirty water to remove the plug. No outlet plug or overflow hole was visible, just slots in the back of the bowl near the bottom. By recessing lift-up wastes into the tray area greater bowl space was gained.

13

This rectangular soap tray with raised ribs allowed air to flow under the soap to prevent jelling.

Flat-topped washbasins marked the first step towards creating bowls within an easy-to-clean, joint-free surface. With the introduction of fixed baths, bidets, washbasins and WCs, separate bathrooms replaced washing tables in bedrooms. Washbasins became smaller as they replaced large, marble-topped wooden cabinets with bowls in bedrooms.

Soap trays

The popularity of more modestly sized bathrooms encouraged potters to expand their washbasin ranges and broaden the variety of designs and decoration they produced. Smaller designs, bow-fronted and corner washbasin styles were added to the large luxury styles. Bowl shapes complemented the washbasin style, with round, oval or rectangular configurations. Soap trays were features which presented artistic licence to the modeller, transferrer and hand-painters. A wide range of soap trays was available, from plain white raised flutes to attractive shell-shaped designs. Soap trays were easy to form by pressing clay into plaster of Paris moulds during production of the washbasin. Soap trays could be recessed or raised. In basins without overflows, holes were often punched into or behind the soap tray, allowing water to drain away.

Above: *An Edward Johns flat-topped, concave-fronted washing table to fit on to a wooden cabinet.*

Below left: *A flat-topped cabinet stand. The washbasin has a tiled splashback and is supported on a cast-iron frame painted to match the bathroom decoration.*

Left: *An Athena cabinet-stand washbasin with a flat-topped raised back to accommodate the cast-iron shelf and mirror arrangement. Cast iron could be formed with imitation carving and painted to simulate the appearance of mahogany.*

Above left: *Drain holes in the soap trays acted as safeguards to prevent the washbasin from overflowing.*

Above right: *A washbasin with overflow slot on the tray behind the recessed lift-up waste control.*

Left: *Splashbacks and side arms were incorporated to prevent water from splashing on to the walls.*

Splashbacks and side arms

Raised surrounds behind and alongside bowls were incorporated into flat-topped washbasin designs. Initially upstand splashbacks had flat upper edges, allowing shelf or mirror units to sit directly on top. The side arms featured curved top edges flowing down to the front *fascia*. When fashion dictated that framed mirrors should be at face level, splashback tops could be curved to match the side arms. The initially straight-shaped top edge of integral splashback upstands evolved through a single central curve, to three, four or even six undulating curves.

Below left: *A Johnson Brothers washbasin with four curves on the back and with bowed front.*

Below right: *A Twyford washbasin, c.1880, with three curves on both the back and side arms.*

TWYFORDS

British Reg. Design
No. 1548 P/1

Size 26" × 22"
(66 × 56 c/m)

"Duramant" Heavy White Ware

Far left: *A Twyford 1920s shelf-top washbasin, raised above the bowl.*

Left: *A washbasin supported on pottery legs with an anti-splash rim around three-quarters of the bowl. The pottery splashback, shelf and brackets above the bowl provided protection for the wall and space for accessories. A 1920s British export, fitted in the Hôtel du Jeu de Paume in Paris.*

Shelves

In the early twentieth century loss of tray or shelf space on smaller washbasins was compensated for by designs with an integral shelf above the bowl. These complicated shelf-pattern basins were more costly to make and only the wealthy could afford them. In the late 1930s a large luxury washbasin, 36 by 20 inches (90 by 50 cm), with shelves at each side of the bowl sold for around £10 5s. A separate matching pottery dressing table for toilet sets and dry cosmetics was also available. Compared with these luxury bathroom fixtures, a smaller, 22 by 16 inches (56 by 40 cm), washbasin of the sort fitted in council homes cost 18s 6d, and a washbasin popular with the middle classes, 27 by 22 inches (69 by 56 cm), cost £2 16s. Single-colour glazed ware was at least a third more expensive than white. (These prices should be judged against the value of £500 for a semi-detached house in 1930s Britain.)

Below: *A Twyford 1929 luxury washbasin with an anti-splash rim around the bowl and twin side shelves.*

Below: *An Edward Johns shelf washbasin, c.1920s.*

Left: *The potters' shop at Twyford's Cliffe Vale factory, c.1924, with a double-bowl washbasin and twin-shelf pattern in the course of being made in the clay state.*

Above: *A Twyford 1930s luxury washbasin, 36 by 20 inches (90 by 50 cm) with anti-splash rim, price £10 5s.*

Left: *An Armitage Ware shelf washbasin and pedestal, typical of the 1930s.*

Supports

Painted cast-iron legs were rough-surfaced and tended to rust or discolour. Pottery supports to match washbasins were introduced at around the beginning of the twentieth century to replace cabinets and cast-iron frames. Pottery supports had an advantage in that they could be easily cleaned with a damp cloth. Large washbasins required two or, if clear of the wall, four leg supports, but smaller designs were stable on a single central pedestal. Oval pedestal washbasins were popular in the early decades of the twentieth century: these elegant washbasins stood clear of the wall on robust central pedestals secured to the wall by stabilising brackets.

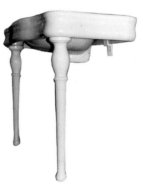

Above: *The underside of the large twin-shelf washbasin with wipe-down pottery legs.*

Above left: *A Doulton 1900 Art Nouveau pedestal washbasin with lever-action taps and lift-up waste.*
Above right: *An Edward Johns luxury oval pedestal washbasin, secured to the wall by concealed brackets.*

A Cauldon bidet with water supply from the rim, lined with blue and gold for French markets.

Bidets

The wealthy classes had seen and used bidets whilst travelling on the Continent, but the bidet attracted minimal interest from the majority of ordinary citizens in the United Kingdom or North America. Many reasons have been suggested for this lack of enthusiasm: the most likely reason is that Allied troops in the First World War who frequented French or Belgian brothels would have been expected to cleanse themselves on bidets before and after associating with prostitutes, and there was a stigma attached to bidets. Yet bidets were standard fixtures in most Continental bathrooms at the time.

Bidets were introduced into South America by French, Portuguese and Spanish colonialists. In contrast to Britain and North America, most South American states considered bidets essential fixtures to complete bathroom suites. Today, although British and American makers continue to promote bidets in their home markets, the majority are exported.

Left: *A combined bidet and foot bath with hot and cold valves to fill the bowl through the rim.*

Below: *An Ideal-Standard bidet with hot and cold valves and directing control from the rim to the ascending spray.*

Above: *A Royal Doulton bidet, c.2001, with soap tray and two metal towel rails.*

Baths

Greek and Roman baths were a tapered, coffin shape – many even served both functions. Fashioned in marble, stone or terracotta, many ancient baths are displayed in museums around the world. The length (usually 60 inches or 150 cm) and the inside shape of baths has changed little over the years. Early English tapered baths were made from sheet zinc or copper. Nineteenth-century cast-iron technology permitted industrialised bath production. The first cast-iron baths were painted inside and out to prevent rusting but the problem with the painted enamel finish inside the bath was that the hot water softened the top coating, leaving the sticky surface adhering to bathers. Early attempts to finish cast-iron baths with *stove enamel* proved difficult.

Many potters continued to make small baths for the legs and feet, but the larger baths were beyond the limits of traditional ceramic materials then in use. Several potters responded to the challenge with the introduction of *enamelled fireclay* baths. They produced baths of 60 or 72 inches (150 or 183 cm) in refractory *fireclay* material with a white enamelled glaze finish. The hard-wearing, easy-to-clean fireclay bath's glazed surface was preferred to the painted cast-iron finish. Like their ancient Greek predecessors, early fireclay baths remained coffin-shaped but these were gradually replaced by parallel-sided baths, which fitted better against bathroom walls.

Above: *A Spode leg-and-foot bath, c.1820, transfer-decorated in Lange Lijsen pattern.*

Left: *Several round-ended fireclay baths supported during drying in Twyford's Bath Making Workshop, c.1924. Baths can be seen in various stages of production, some white to the rim, with roll-edged patterns, white inside and out.*

19

A fireclay bath with wooden rim seat and enclosure; the step stool helped entry and exit.

A round-end, roll-edged bath, 6 feet 3 inches (1.9 metres) long, white-glazed inside, with the outside painted green to match the bathroom décor.

Most fireclay and metal baths were totally enclosed in wooden surrounds. The unglazed top edges of fireclay baths were drilled with leaded screw holes for attaching wooden copings. Early fireclay baths were white-enamelled inside but left unglazed outside so that after installation they could be painted to match the bathroom decoration. In the 1890s embossed floral garlands became decorative features of free-standing fireclay baths; these were often white or coloured to contrast with the clear glazed base colour. At the beginning of the twentieth century roll-top edges replaced wooden rims on baths, and all exposed surfaces were white-enamelled, dispensing with wooden enclosures. Marble effects and raised decorations fired on to fireclay baths matched other bathroom ware. The fired-in permanent decorative motifs on fireclay baths were copied in paint applied through stencils on the outside of much cheaper cast-iron baths.

A colour-decorated, round-end, roll-edged fireclay bath with matching shelf and upstand.

Left: *A Twyford 1896 roll-rim wooden-edged bath with marble-style decoration.*

Below: *The surface paint inside early cast-iron baths softened when filled with hot water. The decoration is in paint stencilled on to a ground coat. The waste and overflow stand tube and trap are exposed at the front.*

Because of the heavy weight of fireclay baths upper floors often required reinforcement before the bath was installed. The solidity of fireclay baths, with their white or coloured glaze to match other bathroom fixtures, had a luxurious, high-quality appearance. This and their high price ensured that mainly wealthy home-owners had them installed. Because of their good heat-retention properties, fireclay baths were also installed in public baths, which were much used by people who had no bath in their own home.

Above: *Sitz baths similar to this cast-iron pattern were also made in fireclay. The bather sat with his or her legs and feet over the front and controlled the water supply through a back or base spray.*

Left: *In the 1950s fireclay for baths was replaced by cast iron, steel and plastic. This free-standing plastic bath, c.2000, stands on a wooden frame clear of the wall.*

Decoration and design

Early washing bowls were made of twice-fired white earthenware, providing an ideal surface for decoration by transfer or hand-enamelling. The earthenware body used in the making of wash bowls was identical to the material used to produce tableware. Transfer-decorated tableware was well established when WC and wash bowls were introduced, and painted or transfer decoration was often applied to white pottery wash bowls in order to enhance their appearance. Depending on the type of decoration, several additional *enamel kiln* firings were required for transfers, hand-painted colours and gold.

Decorative transfers were printed in single ceramic colours from engraved copper plates, an expensive process that had first been used in the mid eighteenth century. Even though the engraving process was costly, transfer decoration was far less expensive than hand-colouring. In order to keep costs down, transfer designs were adapted to fit several styles of tableware and wash bowls. Blue transfer prints were most popular, but pink and sepia tones were also widely used. Specialist printers later supplied potters with multicoloured transfers of flowers and birds. There were also realistic marble effects produced in a variety of colours.

A high level of skill is required to fit transfers around washbasin fascias, bowls and soap trays. Hand-painters often used transferred outlines as guides to paint in with ceramic colours. Gold or coloured detail was hand-painted on to soap trays and overflow shields to enhance the designs. The gold decoration was

A Victorian quarter-size approval model, completely hand-decorated, later used as a sales sample.

Above: *Johnson Brothers sepia transfer decoration with the soap trays hand-painted and lined.*

Above right: *The same sepia transfer was repeated as a painting guide on this bow-fronted basin, with additional colour added to the flowers and leaves by hand.*

Above and left: *Details of soap-tray modelling, transfer and hand-painted treatments.*

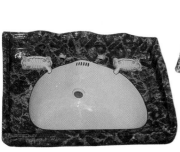

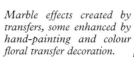

Marble effects created by transfers, some enhanced by hand-painting and colour floral transfer decoration.

normally the final process and required firing at a lower temperature, after which the fired gold had to be *burnished* by hand to brighten the gilded finish.

Towards the end of Queen Victoria's reign the popularity of coloured floral transfer decoration on sanitary pottery waned and gradually went out of

Hand-painted decoration from the 1880s to 2000.

fashion. The new style at the beginning of the twentieth century was *Art Nouveau*, whose sinuous lines translated well into the ceramic process. The style was short-lived, however, and very few examples of Art Nouveau decoration remain.

By the early twentieth century most embossed decoration was being replaced by the new vogue for smooth, rounded styling. Transfers and ornate decorative styling were replaced by modernist white purity of form, with easier-to-clean bowl fronts, corners and edges. Single-colour enamelled and decorated washbasins were introduced by several manufacturers at the start of the twentieth century.

Below left: A small corner basin encased in a purpose-made mahogany furniture unit.

Left: Transfer-decorated corner washbasins were used where only minimal space was available.

A corner washbasin with concealed overflow, recessed under the tap tray.

A Doulton corner washbasin with relief-decorated front fascia.

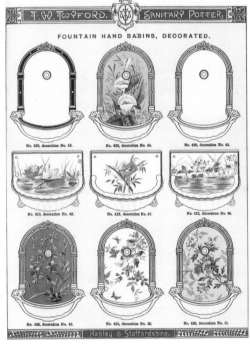

Above: *A Doulton bow-fronted washbasin with roll rim and decorated fascia.*

Right: *1888 fountain hand basins, transfer-decorated on single-colour backgrounds.*

Left: *A Rococo-style corner washbasin with classic fluted pedestal and waste operated by a lift-up rod.*

Below left: *An oval washbasin with marble-effect shading made by coloured glaze over white.*

Left: *The sponge-dabbed colour glaze on the rim flows into the bowl, creating a marble effect.*

A 1926 washbasin in the popular Art Deco sunburst style.

Left: *A Villeroy & Boch prestigious green glazed Art Nouveau pedestal washbasin with cream bowl; made in Dresden, Germany, c.1900.*

Left: *An Art Deco washbasin with angular front and sunburst overflow, c.1930.*

Below: *An Art Deco flat-topped, cut-corner washbasin and taps, 1929.*

Left: *An Edward Johns pedestal washbasin with sponge-applied marble-effect decoration in single-colour glaze.*

Rounded edges remained popular in reaction to the angular Art Deco style, as seen on this 1938 Swiss Laufen basin.

In the mid 1920s Edward Johns began producing single-colour glazed bathroom ware, and other British manufacturers quickly followed suit. The sharp, angular shapes of the Art Deco style, with starkly contrasting black and white glazes, enjoyed limited popularity in the 1920s, a favourite motif being the *sunburst* design. The cut-corner shape of Art Deco influence lasted from the mid 1920s until after the Second World War.

Marble effects had a limited revival in the 1920s and 1930s; rather than using transfers, the ceramic colour was dabbed with sponges or poured on to white glazed ware before further firing.

The utility restrictions imposed after the Second World War reflected pre-war design styles. Dated colours and old designs provided the only luxury bathroom fixtures for British householders. A British Standard specification for washbasins was based on the British industry's most popular sizes – 22 by 16 inches (56 by 40 cm) and 25 by 18 inches (63 by 46 cm). British Standard BS1188 was written in co-operation with the sanitaryware industry to detail the essential plumbing dimensions and overall size of washbasins. Post-war British industry was fighting for a share of the North American market, but bathroom fixtures were rationed in Britain. Special designs for export markets were neither available to, nor thought suitable for, the British market. Choice was limited and the industry's production capacity was unable to satisfy demand.

Above left: A German Standard yellow rectangular pedestal washbasin with softer corners and edges, 1939.

Above right: A Twyford Labvex single-tap hand-rinse basin, c.1930s.

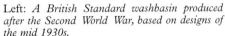

Left: A British Standard washbasin produced after the Second World War, based on designs of the mid 1930s.

Right: *Victor Pimble's 1950s design of a Twyford washbasin made for the North American market.*

Materials and production processes

Volume production of bowls for washbasins, WCs, bidets and bathroom accessories could easily be made from the earthenware or *stoneware* bodies used in the manufacture of tableware. At the beginning of the twentieth century it was difficult to retain the shape of large flat-topped pottery washbasins in the firing kiln as they tended to become distorted. When larger, more ambitious designs were introduced, stronger raw materials were required to hold their shape in the firing kilns. Stoneware and fireclay are both strong raw materials but have a poor colour when fired. In order to make them acceptable to Victorian taste, the body materials had to be blended with whiter minerals or covered with an *engobe* undercoating of white earthenware fused into the natural buff colour. The resultant washbasins were strong, white and comparatively free from distortion, with hard-wearing glazed surfaces that could easily be wiped clean.

Fireclay can be made in thick sections strong enough to retain the shape of large items such as washbasins, baths, kitchen sinks and urinals. The fireclay bath body was capable of resisting distortion during high-temperature firing owing to its substantially increased body thickness. The production process that involved the manufacture of such large fireclay patterns formalised the separation of the sanitary pottery sector from its tableware cousin.

Fireclay baths matched the surface of other bathroom fixtures but were much heavier than cast-iron pieces. Fireclay was used in Britain for the manufacture of luxury baths until the 1950s, when lighter and cheaper cast iron, steel and plastic completely replaced its already small market share. Steel and plastic baths dramatically reduced the weight and cost factors, bringing bath prices within the reach of low-income householders; plastic baths rapidly

Sections through washbasin rims. (From left to right) Solid pressed earthenware; pressed stoneware; pressed fireclay; slip-cast earthenware hollow box; and all bowl vitreous china.

expanded their market share, at the expense of cast iron.

Improved ceramic technology brought about the introduction in the late 1930s of *vitreous china*, a strong, non-porous sanitaryware body, heralding the demise of earthenware and stoneware bodies. Vitreous china became a key factor in the supply of bathroom ware into the North American market. The higher firing contraction of vitreous china, compared with earthenware, stoneware or fireclay, presented an opportunity to introduce new designs, but progress was interrupted by the outbreak of the Second World War. The changeover to the use of vitreous china for washbasin production was finally completed in the 1950s.

Until the beginning of the twentieth century most sanitaryware was formed by *pressing* slabs of clay by hand into plaster of Paris moulds before firing. The *slip-casting* process for washbasins uses a two-part mould. The same method of solidifying a thickness of clay against the mould's internal surfaces is adopted in *hollow* or *flood-cast* sanitaryware. The clay *slurry* builds up on the inner surfaces of the mould; when the surplus liquid has drained away a complete washbasin, with strong, hollow box sections, is formed in one operation. Slip-casting was introduced in 1911 to improve quality, increase the production volume and create stronger products with reduced distortion. By the 1930s pressed production in the sanitaryware industry had almost completely been replaced by the slip-cast process. It enabled the sanitaryware industry to satisfy the huge demand for bathroom fixtures in markets across the world.

Progress since the 1950s

Seeking a share of world markets, the post-war Italian government sponsored its national design industry to promote Italy as the world leader in design excellence. The Italian architect and designer Giovanni Ponti played a vital role in transforming Italy's sanitaryware production from a craft to an industry. Ponti had gained experience in sanitaryware design when he worked at the Manifattura Ceramica Richard Ginori from 1923 to 1930. In 1953 Ponti revolutionised European bathroom design with a new pedestal washbasin for Ideal Standard, Milan. The elegance of Ponti's washbasin made contemporary European designs appear dated.

The interest generated by Ponti's design prompted other designers to emulate his style. British manufacturers brought in consultant designers to work with their experienced modelling staff to create attractive but economically viable designs. The British Design Council helped to promote design excellence for all goods produced by British industry. A new breed of industrial designers worked closely alongside sanitaryware production staff to create aesthetically pleasing styles with commercial appeal to the buying public. Perhaps towards the end of the twentieth

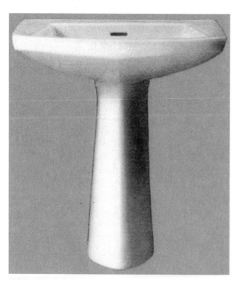 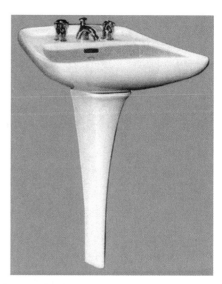

Above left: *An Ideal-Standard, Milan, washbasin of 1953, designed by the Italian architect and designer Giovanni Ponti.*

Above right: *The architect Jack Howe's luxury pedestal washbasin, designed for Twyford c.1955.*

The Twyford designer Alan I'Anson's 1957 Athena luxury pedestal washbasin.

Below: *An Ideal-Standard luxury pedestal washbasin, popular in the late 1950s.*

Above: *The Twyford Sola washbasin won the Duke of Edinburgh Award Design of Elegance in 1962. The design concept was by Stanley Ellis and the Head Modeller was Bernard Grocott.*

century designers pandered too much to the public when they reintroduced and continued to promote nostalgic styles.

Flamboyant Victorian look-alike washbasins reappeared in the 1970s, with a few pieces decorated by colourful transfers or hand-painting. Victorian styling remains popular in Europe and the USA at the beginning of the twenty-first century. The plug bowl has also received a new lease of life. This time the ceramic bowl sits in a lowered worktop with concealed plumbing. Water is supplied from a wall-mounted mixer tap, but if the water is left running the problems the Victorians had with flooding could return: some of the new plug bowls, like their predecessors, do not have overflows.

An Ideal-Standard Art Deco styled Neoline pedestal washbasin.

Above: *A Johnson Brothers luxury shell-styled washbasin with supply-fitting console.*

Above: *The underside of the shell washbasin, showing the trap-concealing shield.*

A Twyford Parmis recessed hand-rinse basin for use in confined WC compartments – the author's design, complying with 1970s Parker Morris standards of government hygiene. The Parmis was still in production at the start of the twenty-first century.

An Ideal-Standard 1970s Cleopatra washbasin for building into countertop bathroom units.

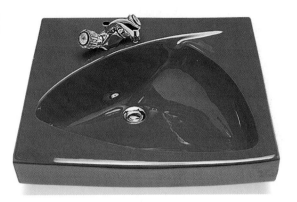

The revised British Standard washbasin retained previous plumbing dimensions and provision for brackets but had a lower back and a swept-front fascia bowl.

Below left: *A Villeroy & Boch free-standing double washbasin by designer Luigi Colani, 1975.*

Below right: *An Italian Catalana simple all bowl pedestal washbasin, c.1980.*

Geoff Kelsall's 1986 angular design pedestal washbasin for Doulton clashed with the contemporary trend to rounded styling.

What about the future? Twenty-first-century bathrooms have come down to us from wash bason stands, then ewers and bowls sitting on dressing-tables in the eighteenth century; washing bowls were then recessed into marble tops and, by the twentieth century, washbasins stood on pedestals independent of furniture. In the 1970s, perhaps in reaction to smooth, modern simplicity, there was a resurgence of Victorian designs and today virtually every sanitaryware maker in the world produces nostalgic reproduction patterns.

An Ideal Kyomi all bowl washbasin, mid 1990s.

Victorian nostalgia: this basin is from the late 1990s.

Right: *The Italian design influence is apparent in this Royal Doulton washbasin for pedestal or waste shield, 2000.*

In the 1890s Art Nouveau was the first conscious move away from the Victorian preference for Greek, Roman and Gothic styles. If twenty-first-century inspiration has to be from history, we could do worse than adopt Art Nouveau styling. In November 2000 ceramic transfers, Art Nouveau freehand painting and relief decoration were created during an artistic design workshop for public exhibition in liaison with Gustavsberg and the Konstfack University in Stockholm, Sweden. The workshop designs were one-off exhibition pieces, but in 2001 at least one international maker offers personalised bathroom fixtures enhanced with unique hand-painted styling. Will a twenty-first-century Giovanni Ponti figure lead us back to plug bowls with wooden cupboards, an Art Nouveau revival, or forwards to a completely new bathroom style?

A Royal Doulton combination of ceramic washbasin with glass shelf and metal towel rails, 2001.

35

Washbasin development through two centuries

A Spode ewer and bowl, Caramanian pattern, c.1809–33. (See page 39 for detail.)

A Doulton plug bowl, c.1830.

A cabinet washbasin, c.1880.

Johnson Brothers decorated bow-fronted and cabinet washbasins, c.1890s.

Art Nouveau, 1900.

Shelf washbasin, 1920s.

Coloured ware, 1925.

Twin-shelf, 1926.

Bowed front, 1930s.

Swiss mixer shelf, 1938.

A luxury twin-shelf basin, c.1935–50.

A cut-corner pedestal basin, c.1940.

A Scandinavian type, c.1950.

A Twyford luxury swept-bowl basin, c.1960s.

A Twyford Sola washbasin, Council of Industrial Design award winner, 1962.

A Twyford Athena luxury washbasin with ergonomic shape for ease of washing.

A Twyford Barbican recessed hand-rinse basin, Council of Industrial Design award winner, 1966.

The Ideal-Standard Kingston, c.1970s.

A Twyford 1970s International countertop washbasin.

'n adjustable-height washbasin, comfortable to use sitting or standing.

A Twyford Italian-style for 2001.

A nineteenth-century plug-bowl theme returns with glass and wood for c.2001.

Glossary

All bowl: a washbasin style where the front rim and sides sweep under the bowl without a fascia.

Art Nouveau: an artistic style which began in 1870 and peaked between 1890 and 1914.

Burnishing: a ceramic process of polishing kiln-fired gold to a bright finish.

Cabinet stand: a cabinet or cast-iron frame to support a plumbed-in washbasin.

Enamel kiln: used to fire colours and gold at lower temperature than primary firings.

Enamelled fireclay: a refractory clay with opaque engobe or undercoat, covered over with white or coloured glaze, then fused into the body.

Engobe: a white ceramic coating to cover the poor body colour of, for example, fireclay and stoneware.

Ewer and bowl: a set for washing comprising a water jug and bowl.

Fascia: the vertical front surface of a washbasin rim.

Fireclay: a strong refractory clay, capable of resisting distortion during firing at high temperatures.

Fixtures: sanitaryware that is plumbed into water-supply and waste services.

Folding tip-up washbasin: a basin fitted to a hinged shelf that when closed discharged the water.

Hollow or flood-cast: a production process in which water is drawn from the clay slurry, leaving a thickness inside the mould.

Lavatory: a term introduced by Thomas Twyford in the early twentieth century for washbasins and adopted throughout the trade.

Plug bowl: a washbasin with a plug outlet in the base.

Plumbed-in: a term describing bathroom fixtures that are connected to supply and waste systems.

Pressing: a production process in which slabs of clay are pressed into concave moulds to produce an item of sanitaryware.

Receiver: a receptacle fitted below tip-up bowls to hold waste water until it drained away or was emptied.

Sanitaryware: pottery providing hygienic facilities for washing in and for waste disposal.

A fireclay corner bath, white-glazed on all exposed surfaces. The damaged area on the rim shows the true fireclay body colour.

A raised splashback washbasin with three back curves and side arms.

Sitz bath: a bath in which the user sits with his feet on the floor and his back supported (from German *Sitzen*, to sit).

Slip-casting: a production process in which liquid clay slurry is poured into a porous mould to make hollow pottery.

Slurry: a mixture of clay and water used for casting hollow ware.

Stoneware: a cream or brown, hard, dense, impervious type of clay body.

Stove enamel: a type of heatproof enamel produced by heating an enamelled item such as a bath in a stove.

Sunburst: a popular Art Deco motif based on the rising sun and its rays.

Table: a trade term used in the pottery industry to describe a flat-topped washbasin.

Tip-up bowl: a washing bowl that emptied by tipping away from the user.

Toilet set: a selection of useful pottery items for personal washing such as bowl, jug, sponge and soap dish.

Upstand: a vertical splashback on a washing table or washbasin.

Vitreous china: a dense, non-porous, white type of pottery for making sanitaryware.

Washbasin: a basin for personal washing, with integral tray and fascia, water supply and waste system.

Wash stand: a frame to support a wash bowl, usually wooden but sometimes in metal.

Waste: the hole through which waste water discharges from the washing bowl.

Water closet (WC): an item of sanitaryware made in one piece of pottery with a water-sealed trap to clear excretion.

A detail of the bowl from the Spode ewer and bowl set shown on page 36.

Further reading

Blair, Munroe. *Ceramic Water Closets*. Shire, 2000.
Evamy, M. *The First Hundred Years*. Ideal-Standard, 1996.
Eyles, D. *Sanitation through the Ages*. Official Architect, 1941.
Lambton, L. *Temples of Convenience and Chambers of Delight*. Pavilion Books, 1995.
Wedd, K. *The Victorian Bathroom Catalogue*. Studio Editions, 1996.
Wright, L. *Clean and Decent*. Classic Penguin Books, 2000.

Places to visit

To ensure that items are on display, it is recommended that interested visitors telephone before travelling.

Gladstone Working Pottery Museum, Uttoxeter Road, Longton, Stoke-on-Trent ST3 1PQ. Telephone: 01782 319232 or 311378. Website: www.stoke.gov.uk/gladstone (The Ceramic Sanitaryware Gallery of this working museum reopened in November 2001, after refurbishment, to house one of the most comprehensive displays of historical bathroom sanitaryware in Britain.)

Science Museum, Exhibition Road, South Kensington, London SW7 2DD. Telephone: 0870 870 4868. Website: www.sciencemuseum.org.uk (Selection of WCs and associated drainpipes.)

Twyford Bathrooms, Lawton Road, Alsager, Stoke-on-Trent ST7 2DF. Telephone: 01270 879777. Website: www.twyfordbathrooms.com (Visits strictly by appointment only.)

Victoria and Albert Museum, Cromwell Road, South Kensington, London SW7 2RL. Telephone: 020 7942 2000. Website: www.vam.ac.uk

A Twyford luxury side-shelf pedestal washbasin of the late 1930s, remaining popular into the 1950s.